Talking to Butterflies and Birds

Meredith Barron

LIGHTNING TOWER PRESS

Talking to Butterflies and Birds by Meredith Barron

Published by Lightning Tower Press, LLC
P.O. Box 381
Shoreham, NY 11786

Library of Congress Control Number:
2025934080

Cover art by Natalie Aller

ISBN 979-8-9865558-5-0 (Print)

Printed in the United States

First Edition: 2025

5 4 3 2

In Loving Memory of Karen A. Wagner

10/20/1956 – 12/8/2022

This book of poems is dedicated to my mom. Losing her has been the saddest, most life-altering experience that I have gone through. Grief for a loved one feels like a big black hole that threatens to swallow you up each day. The process of writing this book provided me with an outlet and a way to communicate with her. The opening poem describes the heartbreak of losing her to cancer in December 2022, two weeks before Christmas. The poems that follow illustrate my attempt to accept her death over the next year and a half. I hope that sharing these words can help others to navigate their grief during an unimaginable loss.

Love you forever, Mom.

Table of Contents

Talking to Butterflies and Birds

Prologue

"*It's the most wonderful time of the year*," except when someone you love is dying.

December ushered in the holiday season, and with it, a new heartbreaking understanding that Mom would be lucky to make it to Christmas. We had celebrated Thanksgiving just a few days prior. Mom rallied, making the best of it for all of us. As Dad, Katie and I talked in hushed tones in the kitchen about the likelihood she would be with us for Christmas, we all agreed that she looked good and hopefully she would. Looking back now, I wholeheartedly believed that. I'm not so sure about my dad or sister.

At the end of October, we had received the sobering news that there would be no more treatments left and that Mom should consider entering hospice. Since then, there had been several changes that signaled she might be nearing the end of her earthly journey. She took all of the medical obstacles in stride, as she had always done, and allowed us to hold on to hope.

But there would be no Christmas miracle for her. I remember going to my parents' house the Saturday after Thanksgiving. A mere two days after she had rallied for the holiday. There was no rally on this day. She sat on the couch, crying out in pain, trying to make conversation between the waves of torture. That was when I realized it probably would not be long. My heart was broken.

I left the house that day with a new sense of dread. She had come close to death more than a few times over the past four years during her grueling battle. But this somehow felt different. It was like skipping to the last chapter in a novel to see how it ends. We all knew she was going to die, but we weren't sure exactly what it would look like or how it would happen.

I returned to work after the holiday and tried to lose myself in the minutiae. I conversed with my students about how their holidays were, clutching tightly to the awful secret that it was probably my mom's last. Instead, I talked about the food we ate, the clothes we wore, and the shows we watched. Afraid if I dared to say the truth out loud, it might become real.

Over the next few days, things started to progress quickly. Mom went from mobile to needing assistance to get from the back bedroom to the couch. Then quickly after, a wheelchair made its appearance. To be soon followed by an oxygen tank and a hospital bed. It was really happening.

The days that followed were a blur. Some minutes felt like hours and at other times, hours felt like minutes. It is wild what your brain will do to protect you from reality when your whole world is crumbling. Most days, I went to work and pretended like everything was fine, only to rush over to my parents' house after to be with her and the family. Even in her last days on earth, Mom was worried about everyone else. "I don't want you taking off work to be over here! You could lose your job!" To make her happy, I looked into FMLA and continued to go to work. I even got observed the morning of the day she died. Our whole world was disintegrating, like a beautiful sandcastle about to be washed away with the ocean tide, but only a few people knew.

As the days continued to drag on and fly at the same time, she got closer and closer to death. We all said our goodbyes more than once, giving her permission to let go, telling her we'd see her again, all while pleading inside for this not to be real.

The night before she died, we sat at her bedside and played her favorite songs. She was no longer able to speak, but she found ways to still let us know she was there. During "Eagle's Wings" a single, solitary tear ran down her cheek. She could still hear us. She was still somewhere in there.

I went to bed that night knowing she probably wouldn't be there in the morning. My goodnight kiss on her forehead lingered longer than usual, I squeezed her hand hard, as I whispered "I love you" and "see you in the morning," even though we both knew that was a lie.

The next morning she would be gone.

Merry Christmas

"It's the most wonderful time of the year,"
except when someone you love just died.

Then, instead, it's a constant reminder of what you have lost.
It's seeing a happy family, smiling together,
picking out their tree, while you cry in the car,
unsure if the tears will ever stop.
It's hearing songs that remind you of your childhood and
Christmases filled with presents and love,
instead cutting like a knife.
You'll never listen to them with her again.
Never see her fingers move with the beat
to pretend she was conducting the song,
Never watch the song light up her smile
on the coldest of winter days.

It's picking out presents for special people,
knowing there will be one less to buy this year.
Your heart breaks as you make your normal list,
minus one.

It's planning festivities with family when
you can't even imagine getting through to the next moment.
"What should I bring?" you ask out of routine,
while the thought of getting dressed seems too much to bear.

It's planning to play Santa for your kids,
while your own heart breaks.
The magic still exists for them, but for you it's gone forever.
Santa cannot bring what you want.
No Christmas miracle to be had for her.

"It's the most wonderful time of the year," but not this year.
The first without you.

One month

Feels like a punch to the gut.
So little I used to think of 1 month, only 30 days.
But now a month might as well be an eternity.
30 days on this earth without you.
Each day I'm further away
from the last day we had together.
Each day adding to this new number of days
that I've lived without you.
How do you live without someone who has known you
and loved you longer than anyone else on this earth?
Someone that literally grew you
from their flesh and blood and sweat and tears?
It's true what they say,
a mom teaches you all of life's most important lessons,
except for learning to live without her.

Pretending

Even the most routine tasks feel heavy lately.
Making small talk with people has never felt so impossible.
"How are you?"
Do you really want to know?
Inside my head, my voice is shouting,
"Don't you know I just watched my mom die?
I don't care about any of this!!!"
But instead I just smile and nod,
I pretend to be ok.
Because it's not their fault and life just goes on,
Without you.

Two months

Two months without you,
And it feels like an eternity.
I collect blissful moments throughout the day
where I think to call you,
Text you,
Talk to you,
Forgetting you won't be there.

These moments are always followed by
The painful realization that you're gone.
My last text to you has already been sent,
My last phone call already ended,
Our last words have been spoken,
Our chance to make new memories in this world has gone by.

As hard as these realizations are,
I hope I never stop "forgetting" that you're dead.
For those moments bring brief seconds of peace,
Where I'm living in a world with you still here.

Marking time

We now keep time not in years but in "befores" and "afters."
"Before Mom got sick."
"After Mom died."
The truth is the days seem to blur past
and go in slow motion all at the same time.

I wish so badly to go back to the "Before Mom got sick."
You were so full of life,
And love,
And dreams.

You loved being a grandma.
You shined so bright with them,
Barely getting 2 years before the first beast came to knock.
I'll never stop thinking of how unfair that was.
Our lives to be forever changed.

The "After Mom got sick" years
had a lot of beautiful memories in spite of it all,
The beast hung over our heads but we made the best of it.
You still loved being a grandma,
Finding new ways to show them your love.

Struggling to find our bearings in this new "after" phase.
I've never felt so lost.
Like the North Star has been plucked out of the sky,
Like time should stand still,
But it continues to march on.

62 days without you

Visits

The last few nights you have shown up in my dreams.
Not in some dramatic way,
Not to tell me that you're ok from the great beyond,
But just as a normal part of my life.

Last night I dreamed that I was in a play,
And you came out to support me.
The night before it was us taking a trip together to the mall,
With your thick brown hair tied back in a low ponytail,
And your bright, unmistakable smile
Spread out across your face.

I know that people believe their loved ones
Show up in dreams to visit
If this is true then the way you're showing up
Makes so much sense.
Interwoven into the most ordinary details,
Always present,
Always reliable,
Always my constant,
Just like you were on this earth.

Miss you too, Mom.
I hope you keep showing up.

Moving on

Time heals all wounds, they say,
Everything happens for a reason, they presume,
But these are just white lies we tell one another
when we're deep in the trenches of grief.

One day you'll feel better,
One day it won't feel so sad,
One day your tears will turn to laughter,
But what if that's not true?

These cliché phrases aren't helpful.
Instead I've created my own motto:
Never moving on, just moving forward,

With you, in my heart, guiding me every day,
Until we meet again.

Life is short

Life is short,
Love is long,
Death is not some unexpected ending.
So why does it feel like it always sneaks up on us?

Like a lioness stalking her prey,
Waiting,
Quiet,
Calculated,
Efficient.

We knew you were leaving,
Yet it still left us gasping for air.
We were preparing to live without you,
But it didn't make it any easier to do.

Death is so final,
And life, so fleeting.

Dark roads

A late appointment meant a drive home in the dark.
Driving home down the same familiar roads
That I've driven so many times before,
But they did not look as I remembered them.
The curves were sharper,
The pavement markings less defined,
As rain fell on my windshield.

The difficulty of this routine task is like living these days.
The most familiar things that I've always done
Seem foreign without you.

Navigating life without you
Is a lot like driving home in the dark,
With rain pouring down.

Pieces of you

When we first found out that you were sick
We started to lose pieces of you,
Little by little,
Not very noticeable at first.
Worry lines formed on your face,
Your voice sounded less steady,
Your words, more unsure.
Faced with your own mortality,
You started to trust less in yourself,
Not knowing what the future would bring.

But as time went on something else happened.
You started to gain new pieces of yourself.
First, a strengthening of faith,
Next, a newfound tenacity,
A strong desire to fight,
A determination to make it to each new family milestone,
And an appreciation for life
Beyond what most could comprehend.

I have never seen so much fight in one person.
An unwavering will to slay the monsters
As they kept coming back.
A relentless perseverance to keep the darkness at bay,
An unconditional love so strong, it surely transcends death.

I will look for the pieces of you in my children's eyes,
I will find you in their smiles.
And little by little we will put ourselves back together.

Missing you

Today I have no clever words,
No deep thoughts,
No inspirational quotes,
Just a gaping hole in my heart.
Today, I just miss you.

Sunrise

A beautiful sunrise this morning,
Reminding me of you,
Hoping you were somewhere
In the clouds and beautiful colors.

Instead of driving into the sunrise,
I had to make a left,
Where the sky was dark and gray and ominous.

This feels a lot like life right now,
Me being pulled further and further away from you
As the days go by,
Too far away to feel your warmth or be
Comforted by your voice.

Into the dark sky I go,
Hoping for cracks in the clouds,
Where your light can shine through.

Wonder

I wonder where you are.
Is Heaven a place in the clouds like they say?
Or is it maybe getting to revisit the best parts of your life?

I imagine you as a child, carefree, running through the fields,
In your wedding dress with your bright smile,
ready to promise forever to your love,
In a hospital gown ready to meet your newborn baby,
On an average Tuesday,
surrounded by little hands and little laughs of your children.
On a Saturday morning,
sipping hot coffee and reading the paper,
In bed,
drifting off to sleep, thankful for the life you have created.

Wherever you are, I know it's beautiful,
Because you're there.

Helplessness

Such a hard feeling to endure,
You stand by and watch your whole world crumble.
You witness your hero deteriorate.
The things that used to take up space on your to do list
No longer seem important at all.

An out of body experience,
As you hold vigil at the bedside
Of the person who brought you into this world,
As you watch them prepare to leave it.

You beg in your head for things to be different,
But aloud you say things like "it's ok if you have to leave,"
Your soul ripping to shreds with each new realization
That this is the end.

Why did it have to be this way?
A question I don't think I'll ever stop asking.

Old soul

I've always loved the term "old soul,"
The idea that souls can live many lives,
In many different worlds.

Was your soul old or young when you were with us?
And are you already living another life?
Or reflecting on the one you just finished?

Combing through memories and conversations,
Trials and triumphs,
Tragedies and miracles,
Looking for the lesson in each,
To take with you to the next life.

I hope that you remember more good than bad,
More joy than pain,
More love than loss,
And most of all, I hope you remember us,
Until our souls meet again.

Three months

90 days,
Countless hours,
Christmas without you,
New Year's without you,
Valentine's Day with one less card to buy,
Dad's birthday with your empty recliner,
And a vacant place at the table,
An irreparable break in our hearts.

90 days and miss you more than ever.

Balancing act

Such a fine line between hoping and knowing,
Praying and planning,
Fighting to stay and letting go.

We hoped you would get better,
knowing deep down it would take a miracle.
We prayed for good news,
trying to plan for the worst.
You fought so hard to stay,
But in the end we had to let you go.

Now it's another balancing act;
How long to stay in the darkness.
I feel closer to you in the sadness,
As if mourning you keeps you closer.
And laughing is leaving you behind.

March 16th

3 years ago today you went into the city to have major surgery,
Just as the world was shutting down.
I kept thinking how miraculous it was
That you got in before everything stopped.
While the whole world took on Covid,
You took on cancer too.

That would mark the beginning of a new journey for us all.
One filled with so many unknowns,
Endless tears,
And so much time apart.

Covid took so much from us,
Cancer stole whatever was left.
Moments we can never get back,
Milestones we will never together get to meet,
Love we will have to send up to the sky instead.

Will

Thought of you my whole run today.
As I struggled to find a rhythm,
I thought about giving up several times.
Then you would pop into my head.
And how you basically ran a marathon every day
For the last 3 years.
Pushing through the pain,
Suffering through hospital stays,
Enduring countless surgeries,
Endless rounds of chemo,
And yet, you always showed up,
And tried to smile.
Willing yourself to survive.

When I'm running, I feel close to you.
I can hear your voice in my head,
Reminding me to push through,
Telling me not to give up.
You didn't quit,
And neither will I.

Energy

"Energy can neither be created nor destroyed,"
A wise person once reminded me
When I had suffered a horrible loss.
A reminder that someone's energy doesn't burn out
When they leave this earth.

I like to think that our loved one's energy
Gets spread out amongst those that they are leaving behind.
I imagine you in my daughter's eyes,
Shining the brightest green when the light hits just right,
In my son's belly laugh when things are going exactly his way,
In the middle of a long run
When I feel like I'm flying and could go on forever.

I miss your physical presence so much,
But I know you didn't just go away.
I'm learning to look for you in different places,
Starting to feel your energy in the most ordinary of spaces,
And it's heartbreakingly beautiful.

Easter

And 4 months since you slipped away from us,
Even though you didn't want to go,
Even though we knew we couldn't live without you,
But here we are.

You loved picking out their outfits,
And spoiling them with baskets and gifts.
We're doing our best to keep your traditions alive,
I hope you can see it from wherever you are.

Last Easter we didn't even get to be together,
So I guess the memories from the year before will have to last.
We were robbed of so much time,
None of this feels right without you,
Not sure if it ever will.

Spring

Spring is here,
Everything is in bloom,
So much that was previously dead and sleeping
is coming back to life,
How I desperately wish that you could too.

Always with you

Always with you, so they say,
And I know this to be true.
But I am also very much without you,
Expected to now navigate the world without a compass.

The ache for your physical presence cuts deep.
I wish I could talk to you one last time,
To hug you and breathe in the way you smell,
To wake up one more day knowing
that you still walk this earth.

Always with you,
But they don't know how empty I feel,
Without you.

Whisper

Sometimes grief is a whisper,
A barely audible "I miss you so."
Sometimes it is a voice yelling so loud
That you can't even hear yourself think,
But it is always there.

It doesn't care if it is uninvited or unwelcome,
It shows up for the big events,
And everyday moments too.
An empty chair at graduation,
A routine phone call that now can't be made,
Your eyes scouring the room for your person,
But not being able to find them anywhere.

They say that grief is just love with nowhere to go,
And I feel that in my bones.
I'll never stop loving or missing you,
So I guess this grief is here to stay.

Chasing healing

Lace up,
Out the door,
Feel the sun on my face,
Earth beneath my feet,
Wind at my back,
I'm chasing healing.

That feeling when both your feet are off the ground
At the same time,
When your breath matches your stride,
Exhaling the pain,
Breathing in new life,
I'm chasing healing.

Those waves of peace
Even though your whole world could be falling apart,
The magic in the mundane,
The silence where I think about you.

Time

What if we all walked around
with tiny hourglasses on our backs
to remind us of our mortality?
Would it help to see the sands of time running through?
To know how long we will walk this earth?
To see when someone only had a handful of grains left to fall?

Would we be kinder?
Would we love more?
Would we appreciate each minute?
Or would we ignore even the most obvious reminder?

Both the gift and curse of being alive is that it is only
temporary.
If you live in fear you're wasting the present,
But if you don't fear death at all,
how will you make sure to truly live?

Tricks

Grief can play tricks on your mind.
It can make the sunniest of summer days
Feel like you're in the middle of a hurricane.
Make you feel all alone in a crowded room full of people.
Looking at your own face in the mirror
And all of a sudden a stranger is staring back.

The life you lived before they died, a distant memory.
Looking at pictures and wishing to go back,
Your heart saying,
surely you'll turn a corner and see their face again,
Reality breaks through to remind you that you won't.

In the beginning there were moments
Where I'd forget that you were dead.
Those don't come much anymore.
I miss those tricks that grief would play.

Holes

Every happy memory created from here on out has a hole.
Sometimes it's an obvious, gaping hole
Felt by everyone in the room.
Sometimes it's only noticeable to a few.
An empty chair,
A missing voice in the joyful chorus of "Happy Birthday,"
One less card to read,
One less hug "hello,"
One less "love you" to be said at the door.

Glimmers

A rough night of missing you,
A simple request to sign up for parent-teacher conferences
Sent me right back in time.
Last year, I rushed home and back from Belle's
To be at your side,
The night you died.

Then today, little signs,
The headband I was looking for
Right on top of a huge pile of clean laundry I've yet to fold,
The most beautiful sunrise with pinks, yellows, and orange,
Hitting the crosswalk with the walk signal on twice,
Feeling the wind at my back on my run's last mile
When I felt so tired.

Hi Mom.
You're not here anymore,
But you're not gone either.

Nine months

9 months without you.
The same time it takes to grow a whole other human life.
The same amount of time I spent floating around inside you,
Eyes closed, waiting to meet you.

It's hard not to think about this stark comparison,
Birth and death,
Beginning and ending,
Possibility and finality,
They are so opposite.

9 months when you're growing life seems like a long time,
9 months when you're mourning one might as well be an
eternity.

Wind

Felt the wind at my back again today at the end of my run.
Was it you
Pushing me forward
When I thought I couldn't take another step?
Felt the warm sun hit my cheek on an otherwise frigid day.
Was it you
Telling me you were there with me?
Felt a calmness come over me as I drove home.
Was it your
Soul saying hi?
I look for you in new places,
As the old, familiar ones remain empty without you.

NYC

One month from today
I will attempt to run the NYC marathon.
A bucket list goal
That I hadn't dreamed possible until recently.

I wish I could say that this goal
Has been purely unselfish in nature,
In reality it is probably more of the opposite.

I felt so helpless when my mom was sick,
Not being able to do anything while she was suffering.
Fighting an invisible, but very formidable, beast,
Watching from the sidelines as our whole world crumbled.
I never wanted to feel like that again.
I wanted to do something.

When I discovered the option to run with Fred's Team
And raise money for MSKCC, I took a chance and applied.
I wrote about my mom.
Her fight,
Her unwillingness to give up,
And the gaping hole that her death has created in our lives.

Training for this goal has meant time away from my family.
Missed soccer games,
Early bedtimes,
Squeezing in runs whenever and wherever I can.
Lots of time alone,
Lots of one sided conversations with her.

Whatever happens on November 5th
I know I can be proud of the work I put in,
And I will be forever grateful
For my family and friends that supported me.
Thank you all so much.

This one will be for you, Mom. Love you forever.

The last "first"

Thanksgiving will be the last of the obvious firsts without you.
How can it be?
It seems like yesterday you were right here.
Yet, it's been an eternity
Since I squeezed your hand or heard your voice.

Last year, we took as many pictures as we could,
I tried to memorize the lines of your face,
The way you said my name,
All while still believing, hoping,
That it wouldn't be your last.

We said grace like always,
Tears welling up in everyone's eyes,
Knowing that what we were grateful for this year
Would probably be ripped away before the next.

My kids will remember that Thanksgiving with their grandma.
Not fully understanding the strength that it took for you
To push through,
To put on a brave face,
To smile and make the memories,
To be grateful,
All the while,
All of us knowing,
It would be your last.

Thanksgiving

We made it through the "last first" without you.
You weren't there,
But you were everywhere.

This will make sense to anyone who has lost someone
They truly can't live without.
You were there in the gold tablecloth set out under the food,
In the guacamole platter shaped like a pineapple,
In the decisions of what to heat up first
And how to organize the oven,
In the words of grace
And the dinner conversation that followed,
In every smile and laugh that we had.

We still hear your voice guiding us,
Your mark forever imprinted onto our hearts,
You're interwoven into every ordinary detail,
Your DNA still courses through our blood.

You weren't there,
But you were everywhere.

2022

2022 was the year of lasts.
The last time I held your hand.
The last time I heard your voice.
The last time I told you I loved you.
The last time I went to sleep knowing
That you still walked this earth.

2023 was the year of firsts.
The first time we ushered in a "new year"
that you would never see.
The first time we celebrated birthdays
with an empty chair at the table
and one less voice in the chorus.
The first Mother's Day without your smiling face.
The first family vacation that you didn't make.

2024 will be the year we make sure you remain.

One year

Well, we got through the year that
we couldn't imagine surviving.
One year since our North Star was
plucked clean out of the sky.
365 days without hearing your voice
or the sound of your laugh,
52 weeks without being able to ask you for advice,
12 months filled with painful "firsts"
and a gaping hole torn through our family.

A year has felt like decades without you here.

My heart both sang and broke the other day
When my kids said,
"I'm getting used to Grammy not being alive."
I want them to heal but not to forget.
I guess that's what I want for me too.
But I will never get used to you not being here.

Gray day

A dreary, dark day,
Washes over me like relief.
A reminder that not every day brings sunshine,
And that even the angels cry sometimes.

Grief

We have become acquainted over the last four years.
I wouldn't call her a friend, but definitely a familiar face.
She was there the first time I heard the word cancer.
Next to me again when you explained that it was stage four.
On the other end of the line when we canceled plans
Because you were sick and scared of Covid.
Right by my side, each time I went to visit you in the hospital.
Holding my hand when we were told hospice
Was the only option left.

They say that Grief is love with nowhere to go.
I get that.
She's also a thief of the worst kind.
She is birthdays never celebrated,
Core memories with someone missing,
Happy days tainted with sadness,
Futures stolen away.

I have no other choice but to love you from afar,
Hoping you can hear me,
Praying you're on the other side of a thin veil,
Right here,
Right next to her,
Right next to Grief.

Bones

"Mom, is Grandma a skeleton?"
Caught off guard by the question of my curious 5-year-old,
Who is always questioning
But has somehow never questioned this.
"No, honey. She's an angel."
Silent for a moment before crafting his next careful question,
"What do angels look like?"
I had to get this right; he always knows when I'm lying.
"Nobody really knows, baby."
His brow furrowed, another question on the way.
"Well, how do you know angels are real if you can't see them?"
Ooof. Another hard hitter.
"I'm not sure, babe. I just believe."
His eyes started fluttering, he'd be asleep soon and I could try
To come up with some better responses by morning.

I thought about his question long after I left him
Sleeping in his room.
You know that crazy pink color the sky can have?
So beautiful that you could never find a crayon to match?
That's the angels.
How I still get to see your face in my dreams, angels.
The one star shining brighter than the rest
In a cold dark winter sky,
The one this same son points to and proudly exclaims,
"Grammy's star!" with a smile on his face, angels.

So one day we all become skeletons,
But what if we become stars too?
I wish we could ask the angels.
I wish we could ask you.

Wrinkles

One of the things that makes me saddest now
Is that I will never get to see you as an old person.
Never get to see more wrinkles on your face
From laughing and days in the sun.
Never get to see the way you might shuffle across the floor,
moving slower than normal,
but carrying so many happy memories with you.
No more days to be spent as a grandma,
No more sleepovers with the kids
or gingerbread houses to create.
We'll never get to see you and Dad holding hands,
hunched over from gravity and years of living,
Like the other couples he always points to while saying,
"me and Mom in 40 years."
How can you miss a memory that you never even had?
I hate this.

Gone

Gone from view,
Gone from reach,
Gone from here.
But where'd you go?

You were just here.
We were just laughing.
Just holding hands.
Living,
In the same world.
But where'd you go?

So hard to feel you
When I can't see you.
So hard to be present
When every moment with you is in the past.

How can you be gone,
When we need you here?

Here

I found ways to talk about you today.
My favorite thing to do.
Bringing you up somehow keeps you here,
Even though you are not.

I told my students how you would always want
To go to Lord & Taylor to shop for prom dresses.
How I would roll my eyes and protest,
"But Mom, they never have anything good,"
And how you would smile and say, "let's just try it."

You always knew what to do,
Where to go,
How to be.
Even though I would push back,
I never questioned if you knew what you were doing.

I know your DNA is entwined with mine,
That because I am here, you are too.
But it's so hard to live without you,
Just really wish you were here.

Skies

I write about the skies a lot.
Maybe because you loved them so much.
Maybe because that's where heaven is supposed to be.

This morning I woke up to the most beautiful sky
Of blues and pinks,
The colors you could never hope to find
In a box of crayons.
I just wanted to keep looking,
Staring,
Dreaming.

But I was already late for work,
So life pulled me in the other direction.
Catching glimpses of the sunrise in my rearview,
I just kept feeling like I wanted to turn back,
But I couldn't.

This is much like grief,
And missing you.
I want to stay in the sadness,
The beautiful colors,
The memories,
Looking back,
To the time when you were still alive.

But life keeps pulling me in the other direction.

I'll try to keep my eyes on the road ahead,
While stealing glimpses of the beauty in the rearview.

Missing you endlessly.
Keep sending us those beautiful skies.

Curse words

It is hard to suffer a loss in a world where "grief" and "death"
Are treated like curse words.
Where people only feel comfortable to utter them
Huddled, in hushed tones,
Afraid that if they say them out loud,
These horrible things might come true for them too.

Dried blood

I have this spot of dried blood under my big toe,
It reminds me of you.
Of the countless hours I ran,
To keep you alive.
Even though your ashes sit in an urn
In the house I grew up in,
Other parts of you are mixed with sand
On beautiful beaches,
And spread into crevices at the bottom of the ocean.

The spot is getting smaller as my toenail continues to grow,
Months later.
Is it weird that I am mourning
The disappearance of this dried blood?
Probably.
But every time I lose something that connects me to you,
I lose you all over again too.

Fragility

Noticed the most beautiful little crocus on our lawn last week.
The deepest shade of purple,
Standing proudly all alone in the grass.
I pointed it out to the kids on our way home from a walk.

Andrew was mesmerized,
"Why is it the only one?"
Quickly followed by asking if he could pick it.
I explained that if we picked the beautiful flower,
It would die.
After a few seconds of pensive thought he agreed
That of course we should let the flower live.
We admired it for another minute or so
Then he said goodbye as we went inside.

On my way out to my car a few days later
I again noticed the flower.
This time it was completely destroyed.
We had gotten hard, heavy rains the day before,
They had just pelted this fragile flower to the ground.
I was so angry.

How long had it taken that flower to grow,
To decide that it had chosen the best time
To erupt from the earth,
To live?
Only to be washed away shortly after.
We wanted it to live,
But nature had other plans.
I was so upset by this because it reminded me of you,
Of the fragility of living,
And how one hard, heavy rain can take it all away.

Jenga

I keep visualizing a Jenga game
when I try to describe losing you.
When you were sick, a piece was removed
and the whole structure shook.
We watched anxiously with wide eyes
to see if the tower would fall.
So many close calls,
But even after countless pieces were taken out,
it was still standing.
You were too.

Until a key piece was pulled,
And it all came crumbling down,
The foundation that we built,
no longer strong enough to sustain
yet another piece being removed.

We watched with tears as all of the pieces fell,
The tower, broken,
As were our hearts.

Trying to rebuild in our grief
is like trying to put the tower back,
with half of the pieces missing.

Ocean

Since I was a little girl my dad has always told me,
"Never turn your back on the ocean."
The phrase has become ingrained,
And I now tell my children the same.

The ocean is powerful, mystical and unpredictable.
Sometimes its waves are huge swells,
And you can barely get up for air,
Other times they are more rhythmic, almost timeable,
And you can duck under them to avoid being tumbled,
And sometimes they are small and calm,
But the undertow is always present.

Went to pick out a card for a friend yesterday
And had to pass by the Mother's Day section.
Although I've already thought several times
About how hard this day will probably be this year,
I didn't account for passing by the cards
And having the realization that this year I won't be buying one.
Felt as if I was knocked down by a huge wave,
While my back was to the ocean.

Eclipse

Slowly watching the sun get covered up today
Reminds me of waiting for you to die.
Little by little, the light in our world dims.
Trying not to look directly at it,
For fear of the damage it will cause.
Complete blackness for some moments,
As the world grows colder and darker.
This beautiful, bright celestial being completely obscured,
You leaving this earth.

Then, a reappearance of the light.
Watching my kids laugh feels like small rays of sunshine.
Hearing your voice in a random video, I feel the warmth.
Seeing you in my dreams, not a cloud in the sky.

We can't always see the sun.
But we know it's always there.
I know you are too.

Patience

It's been 16 months,
Almost a year and a half.
People don't ask much anymore,
"How are you?"
They're over it,
And probably think I should be too.

But for those who have lost someone they can't live without,
It's obvious that's not how it works.
The days fly by and drag on all at once.
Finding joy in little moments,
And sadness in the big ones.

People say *time heals all wounds*,
But I am starting to wonder if they know what it's like
To lose you.
Trying to find patience,
In a world that has very little,
For death,
And its grievers.

Pockets

Picked out your pretty coral denim jacket
To wear to work on a dreary day in May.
It was so bright and so very "you."
I thought it would make me happy.

A few people stopped me,
"I love your jacket, it's so pretty,"
As I thanked them for the compliment and said,
"it's my mom's."

But as the day went on, I realized
I couldn't remember ever seeing you in it.
No memory of how it would have gone with your dark hair,
Or what pants you would have paired it with.
Couldn't picture the necklace
You would have carefully selected to match.

As I thought more about it, it started to make me sad.
Maybe you didn't even get a chance to wear it?

But then I found the tissues.
One tucked away in each pocket,
Unused.
It made me smile.
You must have worn it.

Later, on the way to dance, Andrew asked,
"Mom, do you have a tissue? I really need one!"
I answered him,
As the corners of my mouth turned up ever so slightly,
"I don't, but Grammy does."

Innocence

When you're young things are simple.
People are sick,
They get better.

I hate that my daughter has to ask now with fear in her voice,
"Will I be ok, Mom?"
With any minor illness,
Her voice ascending,
Quivering ever so slightly,
Looking into her eyes,
I can see the innocence lost.

Grammy was sick,
But she didn't get better.
The medicine didn't work,
The doctors couldn't save her.

I loathe that she has to question mortality.
When I was little, I knew people died,
But when they were old and gray,
And sleepy,
And after they had done all they wanted.

I miss our naivety.
And I miss you, Mom.

Texts

Going through old texts today
Because I miss the sound of your voice.
Reading the placement of your words
And exclamation points almost brings you back.
I can imagine you're talking to me.

"Wow, the kids look great!"
"Love you too, honey."
"How's Sharky feeling? All good over there?"

Sometimes I worry I'll forget how you sounded.
Lose the memory of how your tone would change,
Happy,
Sad,
Lecturing,
Wondering.
How you said my name,
How it felt to hear you say everything was going to be ok.

Forecast

Navigating grief is a lot like looking at the weather
And trying to prepare.
Knowing it's raining, we'll put on a jacket with a hood
Or try to remember an umbrella.
If it's cold for the morning
But predicted to be warmer later on, best to wear layers.
For a day with a high UV, get out the sunscreen.

Tomorrow I know I will miss you more than most days.
Watching your first grandchild walk down the aisle
To make her Communion without you will hurt.
Standing in the same church
Where she was baptized 7 years ago,
As you stood proudly by her side will ache.

My eyes will search for you,
I'll have things to tell you.
"Doesn't she look so beautiful?"
Having to imagine what you'd say back
Because I'll never get to hear your voice again.
I'm expecting it.
The forecast says "full of joy" and "full of sadness"
at the same time.

I miss the days of full sunshine,
I miss you.

Ashes to ashes

On almost every run I go on,
I make it a point to run past the crematorium.
This random place,
Less than a mile from my house,
Where we had to leave you.

It was there,
The last time I saw you on this earth,
In a tiny, unremarkable chapel,
With four white walls.
It was there,
Where I said goodbye to you,
And the life I knew before you died.

Is it weird that I hope
That some of your ashes escaped that day?
That somehow they could've blown somewhere closer to me,
Carried by a soft breeze,
Or tangled up in a small pile of leaves?
Is it stupid that I still hope you find your way back to me,
Even though I know you're gone?

"Forever"

We throw around this word
Without respecting its true meaning.
We write things like "Best friends forever" in yearbooks
Of people we won't be talking to a few years down the road.
Say "I'll love you forever" to our first love,
Not realizing this seemingly interminable time
Will come much sooner than we expect.

To learn the true meaning of forever and its permanence,
I had to learn loss.
To say goodbye to the person that raised me.
To wake up every day to raise my own babies without her.
To stare down a lifetime without hearing her ever laugh again.
To be eternally missing a part of me.

When I think about the fact
that I'll never hear your voice again,
I feel like I can't breathe.

"Forever" never seems long enough
When you're dreaming of a happy life,
But it's an unimaginable eternity thinking of one without you.

Faded

Was sitting talking with a friend the other night
About how much I miss you.
Explaining that the traumatic circumstances of your death
Have started to fade.
I no longer picture you frail and weak,
Lines of worry across your face,
Any spark faded from your eyes,
Short, gray hair from the poison meant to cure you.

When I see you now,
You are back bustling around the kitchen,
A big, radiant smile across your face,
The brightness returned to your eyes,
With your thick, beautiful, dark brown hair.

Strangely enough this softening of the edges
Somehow hurts more.
The forgetting of what cancer did to you
makes me miss you more.
Now I have to constantly remind myself
That even though you fought so hard to stay,
That you had to go.

Homesick

I'm homesick,
Not for a home,
But for a person.
Not for a place,
But for a feeling.

For a peace that I had before,
That I can't ever get back.
For a life untouched by loss,
A heart unbroken with all its pieces still intact.
For a time when I could pick up the phone
and hear your voice,
Instead of talking to butterflies and birds.
For the days where I knew where to find you,
And didn't have to chase sunsets and stars.

I'm homesick,
Not for a home,
But for a person.
I'm homesick,
For you.

Lingering

Grief is attempting to clean out your closet
And not being able to get rid of anything.
The sweater she bought you 7 Christmases ago,
The sundress she gave you
because it didn't fit her exactly right,
The t-shirt you bought
at the last beach vacation she made it to,
The work tank that you know you'll never wear,
but reminds you of her.

Grief is trying to move forward,
But wanting to linger in the past,
In a world where she existed,
In the days before it all ached,
In a time when clothes were just clothes,
And losing her was just a bad dream.

"Not really"

You were in my dream last night.
None of it made sense,
Except for the details about you.

You looked exactly as I always picture you.
Your beautiful dark hair, black rimmed glasses and white smile.
I took your hand in mine as we walked.
It felt how it always felt,
Smooth and cold.

We stood for a few minutes together,
Me in front of you
with your arms wrapped around my shoulders.
I asked you how you were feeling,
You replied "I'm ok, hunny."
But I knew.

I asked back, "But not really, right?"
With tears in your eyes, you said, "No, not really."
And then we both stood there,
Silent tears flowing,
Because we knew.

All the times when you were alive and you said you were ok,
But not really.
And all of the times I pretended to believe you,
But not really.

Back

Cried endless tears,
It didn't bring you back.
Ran hundreds of miles,
Still couldn't save you.
Wrote countless poems for you,
Nothing.
Pleaded with the stars to let you come home,
But it was all in vain.

Maybe it wasn't enough.
Maybe I need to try harder.
Maybe I will still do anything
To feel like there is anything left to do,
To bring you back.

Butterflies

I've been seeing monarchs everywhere.
They remind me of you.
You really loved them.

Fascinated with how they would form their chrysalises
In the most beautiful shade of green,
Dusted with the tiniest flecks of gold all along the edges.
How the shell would turn so black and then clear,
Right before they emerged.
Their seemingly enormous wings somehow
impossibly enclosed into that tiny, temporary home they built.

Hoping it's like what happened to you.
Your illness forced changes upon you,
Left you trapped in a blackening cocoon.
But I pray your big, beautiful wings were only tucked
Somewhere up there,
Just out of view.

And now you have broken through,
Like a bright, beautiful monarch.
Free to fly at last.

Miss you so much, Mom.

Meet Meredith Barron

Meredith Barron is a mom, wife, and teacher from Long Island, New York. In this first published collection of poems, she hopes to reach other grievers struggling with the death of a loved one.

www.ingramcontent.com/pod-product-compliance
Lightning Source LLC
Chambersburg PA
CBHW031251120626
46545CB00007B/2761